AN IDEAS INT

Three Keys to Development

Defining and Meeting Your Leadership Challenges

IDEAS INTO ACTION GUIDEBOOKS

Aimed at managers and executives who are concerned with their own and others' development, each guidebook in this series gives specific advice on how to complete a developmental task or solve a leadership problem.

LEAD CONTRIBUTORS	Henry Browning
	Ellen Van Velsor
GUIDEBOOK ADVISORY GROUP	Victoria A. Guthrie
	Cynthia D. McCauley
	Russ S. Moxley

DIRECTOR OF PUBLICATIONS	Martin Wilcox
EDITOR	Peter Scisco
DESIGN AND LAYOUT	Joanne Ferguson
CONTRIBUTING ARTIST	Laura J. Gibson

CCL No. 404
ISBN No. 1-882197-40-2

CENTER FOR CREATIVE LEADERSHIP
POST OFFICE BOX 26300
GREENSBORO, NORTH CAROLINA 27438-6300
336-288-7210

AN IDEAS INTO ACTION GUIDEBOOK

Three Keys to Development

Defining and Meeting Your Leadership Challenges

Henry Browning and Ellen Van Velsor

Center for
Creative Leadership

leadership. learning. life.

THE IDEAS INTO ACTION GUIDEBOOK SERIES

This series of guidebooks draws on the practical knowledge that the Center for Creative Leadership (CCL®) has generated in the course of more than thirty years of research and educational activity conducted in partnership with hundreds of thousands of managers and executives. Much of this knowledge is shared – in a way that is distinct from the typical university department, professional association, or consultancy. CCL is not simply a collection of individual experts, although the individual credentials of its staff are impressive; rather it is a community, with its members holding certain principles in common and working together to understand and generate practical responses to today's leadership and organizational challenges.

The purpose of the series is to provide managers with specific advice on how to complete a developmental task or solve a leadership challenge. In doing that the series carries out CCL's mission to advance the understanding, practice, and development of leadership for the benefit of society worldwide. We think you will find the Ideas Into Action Guidebooks an important addition to your leadership toolkit.

Table of Contents

EXECUTIVE BRIEF

During the course of your career, you are likely to have many different kinds of developmental experiences. You may be assigned to or seek out a challenging position that tests your limits. You may establish a relationship with a mentor. You may feel called to provide leadership for some community activity. Or you may seek out further training and educational opportunities, such as formal leadership development programs. All of these different experiences share a common path — they are avenues toward personal and professional growth. These experiences may make you feel as if your learning and development were accelerated. What caused that acceleration? How do you keep the learning momentum going once the experience ends? This guidebook shows you how to enhance the value and impact of developmental experiences.

Why Seek Assessment, Challenge, and Support?

For most people, the capacity for leadership must be continuously developed over a lifetime of experience. Although people who have or expect to have leadership responsibilities often attend leadership development courses to acquire the needed skills and perspectives, most leadership development happens outside the classroom on job assignments, through relationships with others, or from community service or other experiences outside of work.

At the Center for Creative Leadership, we believe there are three key elements that drive leadership development: assessment, challenge, and support.

Assessment is information, presented formally or informally, that tells you where you are now; what are your current strengths, what development needs are important in your current situation, and what is your current level of effectiveness.

Challenge is elements of an experience that are new and that may call for skills and perspectives not currently available to you; or elements that create imbalance for you and provide an opportunity to question established ways of thinking and acting.

Support is elements of an experience that enhance self-confidence and provide reassurance about your strengths, current skills, and established ways of thinking and acting.

In the leadership development programs we teach and practice at the Center for Creative Leadership, all three elements are present at relatively high levels, creating an intense development experience in a short time. Assessments include personality inventories, 360-degree leadership assessments, feedback from management simulations, and both formal and informal feedback from program staff and fellow participants. Such assessments help you

DEVELOPMENTAL SITUATIONS

UNDERCHALLENGED

- Your skills are almost a perfect match for the demands of your situation.
- Effective performance for a time, but little room for growth.

OVERCHALLENGED

- The demands of your situation are greater than your skills and understanding.
- Substantial demands create high stress and paralysis.

DEVELOPMENTAL BALANCE

- You have a reasonable number of the skills necessary to handle the demands of the situation.
- New skills are necessary to meet new demands, but the challenge provides opportunities for development.

● = Situational Demands   ○ = Current Skills

understand how you are seen by others and how your behaviors impact them. These assessments also act as a challenge in that they can contain new and surprising information for you to accommodate. Further challenges arise within the classroom from staff and fellow participants. A formal classroom also provides support when information presented in the classroom or in class discussion confirms your beliefs, or when materials and exercises are provided that allow you to practice new skills.

These three elements also need to be imbedded in development experiences you have outside the classroom. Without that balance of assessment, challenge, and support, other developmental opportunities are not likely to help you grow as a leader. To drive your development, you must assess your situation and your skills, seek challenges that are developmentally appropriate, and create support for helping you meet those challenges.

Assessment

If you are like many managers, you are probably in a work situation that lacks excitement and learning potential and you need more challenge to help you develop. Or you may be faced with excessive challenges that outstrip the skills you can bring to bear. Your first step is to assess yourself and the challenges you face. Assessment helps you define what you have and what you need. Then you can bring challenge and support into a balance that lets you perform effectively and continue to learn.

When Is Assessment Necessary?

Assessment is necessary whenever your situation changes. In today's work environment, situations can change frequently and abruptly. At a minimum, make an assessment when you take on a new role, when your job changes, when there has been a major organizational change, or when you haven't made an assessment for 12-18 months.

As you plan your assessment, keep in mind these three guidelines:

1. Assess yourself *and* your situation.
2. Use formal *and* informal assessment techniques.
3. Balance self-assessment with data from other sources.

Assessing Yourself and Your Situation

To assess yourself, you will need to collect data on your job performance, your current areas of strength and your development needs, and you will need to understand what you have learned from your experiences. If your company's HR department has access to personality assessment tools, take advantage of those instruments to clarify your preferred learning and behavior styles.

In assessing your situation, you will want to get the best possible information on the key elements of your job or situation; on the desired outcomes or criteria for success; and on key aspects of your organizational environment, culture, or climate. Consider all of the sources that may be available to you, including job analysis, company climate and culture surveys, and talking with colleagues.

You can carry out your assessments either formally or informally. Formal assessments include such sources as questionnaires or surveys used in leadership development programs or the performance reviews used at your job.

Informal assessments include such sources as the feedback you might get (or can ask for) in conversation with peers or direct reports, or insights gained from personal reflection. They also include such things as private reflection or writing in a journal. It is important to carve out some time on a regular basis to reflect on your situation, your skills and development needs, your goals and priorities, and the strategies you are using to handle your situation and achieve your goals.

With age and experience, people can come to believe that they know all there is to know about themselves and their situation, and then be blindsided when their leadership is called into question. One of the most powerful and informative assessment techniques is comparing your self-assessment to assessments from others. Getting feedback from others can seem difficult, time consuming, even threatening. But because self-assessments are often out of line with how others see us, relying on that view alone is deceptive and dangerous. That's why CCL uses 360-degree feedback and other tools to create accurate and effective assessments.

Assessment Starting Points

- Which challenges have I had?
- What lessons did I learn?
- Have I leveraged the lessons adequately?
- Which challenges have I yet to experience?
- Can I get those experiences in my current position?
- What position within my domain can give me those experiences?
- Does my company offer a 360-degree feedback program?
- Does my company provide personality inventory instruments?
- Does my company have an approved outside vendor for assessment services?
- What other tools, such as books, are available to me and recommended?
- Has my company conducted a climate or culture survey in the last year?
- Who else in my organization has been in a situation similar to mine?
- In what areas was I rated highly on assessments by others?
- In what areas was I rated lower on assessments by others?
- How do my strengths and weaknesses relate to performing well in my current job?
- What is my most urgent development need(s)?
- How can I use my strengths to address my development needs?
- What is the most urgent development need I must address for my next assignment?

If You Build It They Will Come

You will be surprised at how differently direct reports, peers, and bosses view your world and the ways they would like you to fix it. Idea boxes, suggestion boxes, and anonymous feedback-to-the-boss boxes can generate a great deal of information. But be careful when creating these informal channels. When people respond, they expect to see change. If you don't adequately analyze and disseminate the information to interested parties with action items, you may damage your credibility.

What Assessment Tells You

As a result of your assessment, you should be able to identify what your current strengths and development needs are, and what your current situation demands of you. Your assessment should also tell you what skills are most urgent for you to improve on now and what skills are less urgent and can be developed over the long term. Finally, assessment can identify if you are underchallenged, overchallenged, or at a point of reasonable challenge, with room for development, in your current job.

If you have had the opportunity to complete formal assessments at a leadership development program or through your organization, look over the information you've collected and search for patterns. This kind of analysis can identify areas of strength and weakness in relation to the demands of your current situation.

Create a table which lists the assessments you've taken, your preferences (on personality assessments) or skills (on a leadership assessment) that seem significant to you, and what that preference or leadership skill means to you in terms of your strengths and weaknesses.

Once you have information on your strengths and weaknesses, you can set priorities. It's important to remember here that you need to pay attention to your strengths and not just your weaknesses. When faced with challenges, you are right to want to improve those areas where you are weak in order to meet those challenges. But you can also leverage your strengths to develop your skills. Combine the information you have gathered on yourself with information you have gathered about what your situation demands. Build a table, like the one below, to set your developmental priorities.

Setting Developmental Priorities

	Important in current job	Not important in current job
Strengths		
Weaknesses		

Challenge

Challenge means you are stretched beyond your current capabilities. Depending on how much of a stretch it is, you may feel comfortable facing a challenge, or you may feel overwhelmed. One thing however is clear: you need challenge to develop new skills and understanding.

Challenge comes from any number of sources. For example, you may be given a promotion with greater responsibility, move to a new department, or be faced with organizational changes like a merger or restructuring. You may receive information that goes against your beliefs, knowledge, or perspectives. Situations outside of work, such as starting a family or dealing with a personal hardship, present their own challenges.

A work situation that challenges you too little carries its own problems. Your company probably hired you and assigned you to a specific position based on your previous success, knowing that you could step right into the job with minimal disruption to the organization. You may perform effectively for a time, but after completing the same type of assignments over and over you are prone to boredom and burnout.

Challenge and Development

Balancing your challenges with assessment and support encourages development so that you can contribute to your own growth as a leader and to your organization while remaining creatively engaged with your work.

If the demands of your job seriously outstrip your skills and understanding, you face a strong chance of failure. Tough demands are not always developmental opportunities. The stress between job requirements and feelings of incompetence can make it very difficult to learn new skills required for success. Faced with this situation, you should increase your support sources to manage and even reduce the level of challenge.

If your skills have outstripped the demands of your job, you should add challenges to your current situation so that you enhance your opportunity to learn and to develop new skills. Otherwise, you become less able to adapt to changing circumstances.

Take some time to write down the challenges you currently face on the job, outside of work, and also possibly in your next job. Write down what you are doing to address those challenges and to prepare for future challenges.

After considering the list you have made, you may see that you have a definite need to bring more challenge to your situation to avoid burnout, stagnation, or derailment. If after considering your list you decide you do not need to add challenge to your current job, refer to this guidebook's discussion of "support" and "keeping your balance."

How to Add Challenge

Challenge and change often go hand in hand. If you make a change to your situation, that frequently brings with it new challenges. Facing those challenges can be a developmental opportunity. The sections following will help you create challenges that will foster your professional development.

Take a new job with broader or different responsibilities than your current one. New experiences, by definition, create challenge. Dealing with the lack of information, the lack of skill, the lack of direction, and the lack of a benchmark that accompany such

❦

changes promotes your development as you deal with experiences for which you are not fully prepared. Making a geographic move or a move into a new organizational culture will also create challenge.

Add responsibilities to your current job. If you can't or don't want to change your position or organization, you can add challenge to your current position by taking on new tasks and responsibilities. Keep in mind that your new tasks should call for skills that make you stretch your abilities and knowledge. For example, if you think you need to rely more on using your intuition when making decisions, add a task that requires you to make quick decisions.

You can make your current job work toward your development in other ways, too. Creating goals that require you to go against the grain of your abilities, such as meeting a deadline despite a lack of resources, or cutting costs when budget constraints are not an acute company problem, can create developmental challenges. Use this list of five strategies to generate ideas about how to add challenge to your position.

• Take on a small project outside your skill area, such as making a presentation for your company in order to develop your public speaking skills.

• Enhance your team leadership skills by managing a group of new employees.

• Build up your soft skills by mediating a disagreement between two other employees, or by establishing a relationship with someone in the office with whom you don't get along.

• Take on a small strategic assignment, such as summarizing the benefits and use of a new organizational technology (for example, an Intranet).

• Teach to become a better learner, perhaps by offering a workshop in your area of expertise at a local library.

Seek new perspectives. Coming to grips with diverse points of view brings challenge to any situation, old or new, as it points to new ways of thinking and new behaviors. As you bring together your views with the views of others, you broaden your understanding of what is possible, available, perhaps even what is true. The following list can point you toward people inside and outside of your company whose views may be different from yours.

• People who work in different functional areas of the company from you.

• People who report to a different organizational level or to a different division.

• People who have a different educational background from you.

• People of the opposite gender.

• People of a different ethnic background or nationality.

• People with religious views different from your own.

• People that stand outside the company's external boundary, such as customers, suppliers, or strategic partners.

Seek responsibilities away from work. There are situations when adding challenge to your current position is not possible. Your organization may consider adding developmental opportunities to your job too risky, for example. You may not have the support you need to successfully add challenge to your current job. In cases like this, taking on new activities outside of work can also provide valuable developmental opportunities. This list suggests outside activities that will help you think of your own opportunities.

• To improve your leadership skills, volunteer to chair a service group or project in your community.

• To bolster your speaking skills, contact a local speakers' bureau for opportunities to present in your areas of expertise.

- Take a course in peer counseling, or volunteer to be a peer counselor, to build up your listening skills.
- Coach a youth sports club to improve your effectiveness in dealing with novices and building teams.
- Serve as an advisor or consultant in your skill area to a group outside of your organization.

Four Ways to Add Challenge

1. Make a job or organization change.
2. Add new tasks, responsibilities, or goals to your existing job.
3. Look for developmental opportunities outside of work.
4. Seek out new perspectives.

Support

It's important that you continue to assess your skills, development needs, and job situation on a regular basis. Periodic self-evaluations can alert you when the challenges you face are too out of line with, or too different from, the skills and personal resources you have. A recent promotion, a company reorganization, a personal trauma such as a family illness—any of these situations and many others can create severe challenges.

Faced with overwhelming challenges, you may be tempted to deny the challenges exist at all. Or you may want to rely on the strengths and skills you have, only to realize that these are not the skills necessary to meet the challenge. The solution to difficult challenges is support—a means of enhancing your self-confidence, affirming your strengths, and guiding your acquisition of new skills needed to meet those challenges.

Increasing Support to Manage Challenges

Building support is key to your managing and even reducing the challenges you face, bringing them in line with your current skills. Increased support will help you reach the point where your situation is more balanced between the challenges you face and the skills you possess. From a strong balanced position you are better able to learn, to grow, and to build skills and perspectives that help you develop as a leader.

How to Build Support

When you think of support, you may think of other people. That is a good place to start, but do not limit yourself to a few close individuals. Support can come from spouses, significant others, bosses, peers or work colleagues, your direct reports, human resources staff, friends, coaches, mentors, fellow community volunteers, religious leaders, or from anyone else with whom you have some kind of relationship.

When considering another person as a source of support, think of the role you want that person to play. Some helpful support roles include:

• Counselor. This person provides emotional support and encouragement and lets you vent your feelings.

• Cheerleader. This person can express confidence in your current abilities and in your ability to learn and grow.

• Reinforcer. This person rewards you for your progress.

• Cohort. This person is in a situation similar to yours, and so can offer empathy.

• Mentor. This is a more formal role than counselor, cheerleader, reinforcer, or cohort. A mentor provides long-term support and guidance through experience and example.

• Coach. Like mentor, this role is also formal. This person provides focused support geared toward your acquiring a specific skill or overcoming a particular hurdle. A coach can also ensure that you get ongoing assessment and feedback on your progress. Your company may help you find a coach, or you can choose your own. If you select your own coach, keep in mind that different people can coach you in different skills.

Finding Support

As you build a support network, keep in mind the different roles you need supporters to play. If you want a coach, for example, look for someone skilled or knowledgeable in the areas in which you are weak, who has successful experience managing a situation similar to yours, or who can help you think through your immediate challenges. Your coach must believe in you as a viable and competent member of the organization and must be willing to invest the time necessary to help you manage the challenges you face. It's helpful if you first identify those skills you need to improve, and anticipate the goal you want to achieve in meeting your challenges. In the same way, identify other supporters by the roles you require them to play and which they are capable of performing.

Challenge or Area for Improvement: _____

_____

Support Role: _____
(counselor, cheerleader, reinforcer, cohort, mentor, coach)

Support Person: _____

Desired Outcome: _____

_____

_____

Challenge or Area for Improvement: _____

_____

Support Role: _____
(counselor, cheerleader, reinforcer, cohort, mentor, coach)

Support Person: _____

Desired Outcome: _____

_____

_____

Challenge or Area for Improvement: _____

_____

Support Role: _____
(counselor, cheerleader, reinforcer, cohort, mentor, coach)

Support Person: _____

Desired Outcome: _____

_____

_____

You are right in considering people as your main source of support as you face challenging situations. But there are also other avenues of support available to you. An important place to look is inside yourself. The language you use inside your head has a great deal of influence over how you see problems and over your attitude toward overcoming the challenges. Clarify your priorities, set and follow through on priorities, and use positive self-talk to develop the self-discipline you need to tackle tough challenges.

You can also build formal and informal support sources from your company's established systems. Look for reservoirs of incentive and encouragement in the following places, to mention a few:

- Reward and recognition policies
- Performance development procedures
- Leadership development systems
- Chain of command
- Policies manuals
- Human resources department
- Employee assistance programs

You might also find support where you haven't thought to look. Books, web sites, videos, and electronic mailing lists can stimulate reflection, personal introspection, new perspectives, and strong emotions. Repeated visits to these resources let you verify their relevance and usefulness. Less obvious but still useful support tools include screen savers and desk reminders, which you can set to remind yourself of goals, to spur yourself toward a deadline, or to suggest that you take time to reflect. Be sure to keep these kinds of sources updated so they stay relevant.

Keeping Your Balance

The best developmental situation you can make for yourself is one in which learning becomes an ongoing element of your experience. Assessment, challenge, and support work together to build that kind of situation. By examining yourself and your situation, you learn which of your strengths are not critical to your current situation, you know where you are skillfully employing your relevant skills, and you become aware of skills you need to develop.

Developing new skills can be hard. Accepting new challenges can make you uncomfortable as you feel less competent than you usually feel. Building support in the face of challenges is key to developing your competence as a leader. Your continued assessment of yourself and your situation enable you to balance your skills and the demands you face. Using assessment, challenge, and support together, you can seize the opportunity found in your current situation to develop your leadership and managerial skills for tomorrow while effectively meeting your responsibilities today.

Suggested Readings

Dalton, M. A. (1998). *Becoming a more versatile learner.* Greensboro, NC: Center for Creative Leadership.

Douglas, C. A., & McCauley, C. D. (1997). A survey on the use of formal developmental relationships in organizations. *Issues & Observations, 17*(1/2), 6-9. Greensboro, NC: Center for Creative Leadership.

Lombardo, M. M., & Eichinger, R. W. (1989). *Eighty-eight assignments for development in place.* Greensboro, NC: Center for Creative Leadership.

McCall, M. W., Jr., Lombardo, M. M., & Morrison, A. M. (1988). *The lessons of experience.* Lexington, MA: Lexington Books.

McCauley, C. D., Moxley, R. S., & Van Velsor, E. (Eds.). (1998). *The Center for Creative Leadership handbook of leadership development.* San Francisco: Jossey-Bass.

McCauley, C. D. (1999). *Learning from work experience: The Job Challenge Profile.* San Francisco: Jossey-Bass/Pfeiffer.

Background

The advice given in this guidebook is backed by CCL's research and educational experience, which has over the years demonstrated the value of (1) assessment for development and (2) systemic development.

Assessment for development has been a focus of CCL since its beginning in 1970. At that time the long-standing practice of the business world, as reflected in the use of assessment centers to identify potential managers, was to evaluate employees to determine whether they should receive assignments but not to tell those employees what was learned about them.

CCL had a different idea. We believed that if you tell people how they are doing, this information can help them do better. This simple but powerful notion was built into the feedback-intensive program experiences developed at CCL.

CCL also understood from the beginning that developing the capacity to lead was not something that could be accomplished by a single, time-limited event. This understanding, shaped by CCL research on how executives learn from experience and by the effort to follow up with participants of CCL programs, has evolved into the recognition that leadership must be developed by means of a continual and systemic process, and that an essential aspect of this process is assessment (through ongoing feedback), challenge, and support.

Key Point Summary

For most people, the capacity for leadership must be continuously developed over a lifetime of experience. At the Center for Creative Leadership, we believe there are three key elements that drive leadership development: assessment, challenge, and support.

Assessment is information, presented formally or informally, that tells you where you are now; what are your current strengths, what development needs are important in your current situation, and what is your current level of effectiveness. Assessment is necessary whenever your situation changes. At a minimum, make an assessment when you take on a new role, when your job changes, when there has been a major organizational change, or when you haven't made an assessment for 12-18 months. As you plan your assessment, keep in mind these three guidelines: (1) assess yourself and your situation; (2) use formal and informal assessment techniques; and (3) balance self-assessment with data from other sources.

Challenge means you are stretched beyond your current capabilities. Depending on how much of a stretch it is, you may feel comfortable facing a challenge, or you may feel overwhelmed. Challenge may call for skills and perspectives not currently available to you, or it may create imbalance for you and provide an opportunity to question established ways of thinking and acting. A work situation that challenges you too little carries its own problems. After completing the same type of assignments over and over you are prone to boredom and burnout.

Support enhances self-confidence and provides reassurance about your strengths, current skills, and established ways of thinking and acting. It can guide your acquisition of new skills. Building support is key to your managing and even reducing the challenges you face, bringing them in line with your current skills. Increased support will help you reach the point where your situation is more balanced between the challenges you face and the skills you possess. From a strong balanced position you are better able to learn, to grow, and to build skills and perspectives that help you develop as a leader.

ORDERING INFORMATION

To order additional Ideas Into Action guidebooks, please contact us by phone at **336 545 2810** or visit our online bookstore at **www.ccl.org/publications**. Prepayment is required for all orders under $100.

Ongoing Feedback: How to Get It, How to Use It (#400) $8.95

Reaching Your Development Goals (#401) $8.95

Becoming a More Versatile Learner (#402) $8.95

Giving Feedback to Subordinates (#403) $8.95

Three Keys to Development: Defining and Meeting Your Leadership Challenges (#404) $8.95

Feedback That Works: How to Build and Deliver Your Message (#405) $8.95

Communicating Across Cultures (#406) $8.95

Learning from Life: Turning Life's Lessons into Leadership Experience (#407) $8.95

Keeping Your Career on Track: Twenty Success Strategies (#408) $8.95

Preparing for Development: Making the Most of Formal Leadership Programs (#409) $8.95

Choosing an Executive Coach (#410) $8.95

Setting Your Development Goals: Start with Your Values (#411) $8.95

Do You Really Need a Team? (#412) $8.95

Building Resiliency: How to Thrive in Times of Change (#413) $8.95

How to Form a Team: Five Keys to High Performance (#414) $8.95

Using Your Executive Coach (#415) $8.95

Managing Conflict with Your Boss (#416) $8.95

How to Launch a Team: Start Right for Success (#417) $8.95

Managing Conflict with Direct Reports (#418) $8.95

Managing Conflict with Peers (#419) $8.95

Feedback Package (#724; includes #400, #403, #405) $17.95

Individual Leadership Development Package (#726; includes #401, #404, #409, #411) $26.95

U.S. shipping (UPS Ground – $4 for 1st book; $0.95 each additional book)
Non-U.S. shipping (Express International – $20 for 1st book; $5 each additional book)
CCL's Federal Tax ID #23-707-9591

Single title quantity discounts: 5-99 – $7.95; 100-499 – $6.50; 500+ – $5.95